THE LORDS and THE NEW CREATURES

poems

JIM MORRISON

A TOUCHSTONE BOOK
Published by Simon & Schuster
New York London Toronto Sydney New Delhi

Touchstone
A Division of Simon & Schuster, Inc.
1230 Avenue of the Americas
New York, NY 10020

This Touchstone trade paperback edition January 2012

TOUCHSTONE and colophon are registered trademarks of Simon & Schuster, Inc.

For information about special discounts for bulk purchases, please
contact Simon & Schuster Special Sales at 1-866-506-1949 or
business@simonandschuster.com.

The Simon & Schuster Speakers Bureau can bring authors to your live event.
For more information or to book an event contact the Simon & Schuster
Speakers Bureau at 866-248-3049 or visit our website at
www.simonspeakers.com.

Designed by Renata Di Biase

Manufactured in the United States of America

60 59 58 57

Library of Congress Cataloging-in-Publication Data
Morrison, Jim, 1943–1971.
    The lords, and The new creatures, poems.
        p.   cm.
PS3563.08746 L6 1970
811'.5'4   74-107256

ISBN 978-0-671-21044-1

CONTENTS

THE LORDS
NOTES ON VISION   *1*

THE NEW CREATURES   *83*

THE LORDS

NOTES ON VISION

Look where we worship.

We all live in the city.

The city forms—often physically, but inevitably
psychically—a circle. A Game. A ring of death
with sex at its center. Drive toward outskirts
of city suburbs. At the edge discover zones of
sophisticated vice and boredom, child prosti-
tution. But in the grimy ring immediately surround-
ing the daylight business district exists the only
real crowd life of our mound, the only street
life, night life. Diseased specimens in dollar
hotels, low boarding houses, bars, pawn shops,
burlesques and brothels, in dying arcades which
never die, in streets and streets of all-night
cinemas.

When play dies it becomes the Game.
When sex dies it becomes Climax.

All games contain the idea of death.

Baths, bars, the indoor pool. Our injured leader
prone on the sweating tile. Chlorine on his breath
and in his long hair. Lithe, although crippled,
body of a middle-weight contender. Near him
the trusted journalist, confidant. He liked men
near him with a large sense of life. But most
of the press were vultures descending on the
scene for curious America aplomb. Cameras
inside the coffin interviewing worms.

It takes large murder to turn rocks in the shade
and expose strange worms beneath. The lives of
our discontented madmen are revealed.

Camera, as all-seeing god, satisfies our longing
for omniscience. To spy on others from this
height and angle: pedestrians pass in and out of
our lens like rare aquatic insects.

• •

Yoga powers. To make oneself invisible or small.
To become gigantic and reach to the farthest things.
To change the course of nature. To place oneself
anywhere in space or time. To summon the dead.
To exalt senses and perceive inaccessible images,
of events on other worlds, in one's deepest inner
mind, or in the minds of others.

• •

The sniper's rifle is an extension of his eye. He
kills with injurious vision.

The assassin (?), in flight, gravitated with
unconscious, instinctual insect ease, moth-
like, toward a zone of safety, haven from the
swarming streets. Quickly, he was devoured
in the warm, dark, silent maw of the physical
theater.

Modern circles of Hell: Oswald (?) kills President.
Oswald enters taxi. Oswald stops at rooming house.
Oswald leaves taxi. Oswald kills Officer Tippitt.
Oswald sheds jacket. Oswald is captured.

He escaped into a movie house.

In the womb we are blind cave fish.

Everything is vague and dizzy. The skin swells and there is no more distinction between parts of the body. An encroaching sound of threatening, mocking, monotonous voices. This is fear and attraction of being swallowed.

Inside the dream, button sleep around your body
like a glove. Free now of space and time. Free
to dissolve in the streaming summer.

Sleep is an under-ocean dipped into each night.
At morning, awake dripping, gasping, eyes
stinging.

The eye looks vulgar
Inside its ugly shell.
Come out in the open
In all of your Brilliance.

Nothing. The air outside
burns my eyes.
I'll pull them out
and get rid of the burning.

Crisp hot whiteness
City Noon
Occupants of plague zone
are consumed.

(Santa Ana's are winds off deserts.)

Rip up grating and splash in gutters.
The search for water, moisture,
"wetness" of the actor, lover.

"Players"—the child, the actor, and the gambler.
The idea of chance is absent from the world of the
child and primitive. The gambler also feels in
service of an alien power. Chance is a survival
of religion in the modern city, as is theater,
more often cinema, the religion of possession.

What sacrifice, at what price can the city be born?

There are no longer "dancers," the possessed.
The cleavage of men into actor and spectators
is the central fact of our time. We are obsessed
with heroes who live for us and whom we punish.
If all the radios and televisions were deprived
of their sources of power, all books and paintings
burned tomorrow, all shows and cinemas closed,
all the arts of vicarious existence . . .

We are content with the "given" in sensation's
quest. We have been metamorphosised from a mad
body dancing on hillsides to a pair of eyes
staring in the dark.

Not one of the prisoners regained sexual balance.
Depressions, impotency, sleeplessness . . . erotic
dispersion in languages, reading, games, music,
and gymnastics.

The prisoners built their own theater which
testified to an incredible surfeit of leisure.
A young sailor, forced into female roles, soon
became the "town" darling, for by this time they
called themselves a town, and elected a mayor,
police, aldermen.

In old Russia, the Czar, each year, granted—
out of the shrewdness of his own soul or one of
his advisors'—a week's freedom for one convict
in each of his prisons. The choice was left to the
prisoners themselves and it was determined in
several ways. Sometimes by vote, sometimes by lot,
often by force. It was apparent that the chosen
must be a man of magic, virility, experience,
perhaps narrative skill, a man of possibility, in
short, a hero. Impossible situation at the
moment of freedom, impossible selection,
defining our world in its percussions.

A room moves over a landscape, uprooting the mind,
astonishing vision. A gray film melts off the
eyes, and runs down the cheeks. Farewell.

Modern life is a journey by car. The Passengers
change terribly in their reeking seats, or roam
from car to car, subject to unceasing transformation.
Inevitable progress is made toward the beginning
(there is no difference in terminals), as we
slice through cities, whose ripped backsides present
a moving picture of windows, signs, streets,
buildings. Sometimes other vessels, closed
worlds, vacuums, travel along beside to move
ahead or fall utterly behind.

Destroy roofs, walls, see in all the rooms at once.

From the air we trapped gods, with the gods' omniscient gaze, but without their power to be inside minds and cities as they fly above.

June 30th. On the sun roof. He woke up suddenly.
At that instant a jet from the air base crawled
in silence overhead. On the beach, children try
to leap into its swift shadow.

The bird or insect that stumbles into a room
and cannot find the window. Because they know
no "windows."

Wasps, poised in the window,
Excellent dancers,
detached, are not inclined
into our chamber.

Room of withering mesh
read love's vocabulary
in the green lamp
of tumescent flesh.

When men conceived buildings,
and closed themselves in chambers,
first trees and caves.

(Windows work two ways,
mirrors one way.)

You never walk through mirrors
or swim through windows.

Cure blindness with a whore's spittle.

In Rome, prostitutes were exhibited on roofs
above the public highways for the dubious
hygiene of loose tides of men whose potential
lust endangered the fragile order of power.
It is even reported that patrician ladies, masked
and naked, sometimes offered themselves up to
these deprived eyes for private excitements of
their own.

More or less, we're all afflicted with the psychology
of the voyeur. Not in a strictly clinical or
criminal sense, but in our whole physical and
        emotional
stance before the world. Whenever we seek to break
this spell of passivity, our actions are cruel and
awkward and generally obscene, like an invalid who
has forgotten how to walk.

The voyeur, the peeper, the Peeping Tom, is a dark
comedian. He is repulsive in his dark anonymity,
in his secret invasion. He is pitifully alone.
But, strangely, he is able through this same silence
and concealment to make unknowing partner of
        anyone
within his eye's range. This is his threat and
power.

There are no glass houses. The shades are drawn
and "real" life begins. Some activities are impossible
in the open. And these secret events are the voyeur's
game. He seeks them out with his myriad army of
eyes—like the child's notion of a Deity who sees
all. "Everything?" asks the child. "Yes, every-
thing," they answer, and the child is left to cope
with this divine intrusion.

The voyeur is masturbator, the mirror his badge,
the window his prey.

Urge to come to terms with the "Outside," by
absorbing, interiorizing it. I won't come out,
you must come in to me. Into my womb-garden
where I peer out. Where I can construct a universe
within the skull, to rival the real.

She said, "Your eyes are always black." The pupil
opens to seize the object of vision.

Imagery is born of loss. Loss of the "friendly expanses." The breast is removed and the face imposes its cold, curious, forceful, and inscrutable presence.

You may enjoy life from afar. You may look at things but not taste them. You may caress the mother only with the eyes.

You cannot touch these phantoms.

French Deck. Solitary stroker of cards. He
dealt himself a hand. Turn stills of the past in
unending permutations, shuffle and begin. Sort
the images again. And sort them again. This
game reveals germs of truth, and death.

The world becomes an apparently infinite, yet
possibly finite, card game. Image combinations,
permutations, comprise the world game.

A mild possession, devoid of risk, at bottom
sterile. With an image there is no attendant
danger.

Muybridge derived his animal subjects from the
Philadelphia Zoological Garden, male performers
from the University. The women were professional
artists' models, also actresses and dancers,
parading nude before the 48 cameras.

Films are collections of dead pictures which are
given artificial insemination.

Film spectators are quiet vampires.

Cinema is most totalitarian of the arts. All
energy and sensation is sucked up into the skull,
a cerebral erection, skull bloated with blood.
Caligula wished a single neck for all his subjects
that he could behead a kingdom with one blow.
Cinema is this transforming agent. The body
exists for the sake of the eyes; it becomes a
dry stalk to support these two soft insatiable
jewels.

Film confers a kind of spurious eternity.

Each film depends upon all the others and drives you on to others: Cinema was a novelty, a scientific toy, until a sufficient body of works had been amassed, enough to create an intermittent other world, a powerful, infinite mythology to be dipped into at will.

Films have an illusion of timelessness fostered by their regular, indomitable appearance.

The appeal of cinema lies in the fear of death.

The modern East creates the greatest body of films.
Cinema is a new form of an ancient tradition—the
shadow play. Even their theater is an imitation
of it. Born in India or China, the shadow show
was aligned with religious ritual, linked with
celebrations which centered around cremation of the
dead.

It is wrong to assume, as some have done, that cinema belongs to women. Cinema is created by men for the consolation of men.

The shadow plays originally were restricted to
male audiences. Men could view these dream shows
from either side of the screen. When women later
began to be admitted, they were allowed to attend
only to shadows.

Male genitals are small faces
forming trinities of thieves
and Christs
Fathers, sons, and ghosts.

A nose hangs over a wall
and two half eyes, sad eyes,
mute and handless, multiply
an endless round of victories.

These dry and secret triumphs, fought
in stalls and stamped in prisons,
glorify our walls
and scorch our vision.

A horror of empty spaces
propagates this seal on private places.

Kynaston's Bride
may not appear
but the odor of her flesh
is never very far.

A drunken crowd knocked over the apparatus,
and Mayhew's showman, exhibiting at Islington
Green, burned up, with his mate, inside.

In 1832, Gropius was astounding Paris with his
Pleorama. The audience was transformed into
the crew aboard a ship engaged in battle. Fire,
screaming, sailors, drowning.

Robert Baker, an Edinburgh artist, while in jail
for debt, was struck by the effect of light shining
through the bars of his cell through a letter he
was reading, and out of this perception he in-
vented the first *Panorama*, a concave, transparent
picture view of the city.

This invention was soon replaced by the *Diorama*,
which added the illusion of movement by shifting
the room. Also sounds and novel lighting effects.
Daguerre's London Diorama still stands in Regent's
Park, a rare survival, since these shows depended
always on effects of artificial light, produced
by lamps or gas jets, and nearly always ended
in fire.

Phantasmagoria, magic lantern shows, spectacles
without substance. They achieved complete
sensory experiences through noise, incense,
lightning, water. There may be a time when
we'll attend Weather Theaters to recall the
sensation of rain.

Cinema has evolved in two paths.

One is spectacle. Like the Phantasmagoria, its
goal is the creation of a total substitute
sensory world.

The other is peep show, which claims for its
realm both the erotic and the untampered obser-
vance of real life, and imitates the keyhole or
voyeur's window without need of color, noise,
grandeur.

Cinema discovers its fondest affinities, not
with painting, literature, or theater, but with
the popular diversions—comics, chess, French
and Tarot decks, magazines, and tattooing.

Cinema derives not from painting, literature,
sculpture, theater, but from ancient popular
wizardry. It is the contemporary manifestation
of an evolving history of shadows, a delight in
pictures that move, a belief in magic. Its
lineage is entwined from the earliest beginning
with Priests and sorcery, a summoning of phantoms.
With, at first, only slight aid of the mirror and
fire, men called up dark and secret visits from
regions in the buried mind. In these seances,
shades are spirits which ward off evil.

The spectator is a dying animal.

Invoke, palliate, drive away the Dead. Nightly.

Through ventriloquism, gestures, play with objects,
and all rare variations of the body in space,
the shaman signaled his "trip" to an audience
which shared the journey.

In the seance, the shaman led. A sensuous panic,
deliberately evoked through drugs, chants, dancing,
hurls the shaman into trance. Changed voice,
convulsive movement. He acts like a madman. These
professional hysterics, chosen precisely for their
psychotic leaning, were once esteemed. They
mediated between man and spirit-world. Their mental
travels formed the crux of the religious life of
the tribe.

Principle of seance: to cure illness. A mood
might overtake a people burdened by historical
events or dying in a bad landscape. They seek
deliverance from doom, death, dread. Seek posses-
sion, the visit of gods and powers, a rewinning
of the life source from demon possessors. The
cure is culled from ecstasy. Cure illness or
prevent its visit, revive the sick, and regain
stolen, soul.

It is wrong to assume that art needs the spectator
in order to be. The film runs on without any eyes.
The spectator cannot exist without it. It insures
his existence.

The happening/the event in which ether is introduced
into a roomful of people through air vents makes
the chemical an actor. Its agent, or injector,
is an artist-showman who creates a performance
to witness himself. The people consider themselves
audience, while they perform for each other,
and the gas acts out poems of its own through
the medium of the human body. This approaches
the psychology of the orgy while remaining in
the realm of the Game and its infinite permu-
tations.

The aim of the happening is to cure boredom,
wash the eyes, make childlike reconnections
with the stream of life. Its lowest, widest
aim is for purgation of perception. The happening
attempts to engage all the senses, the total
organism, and achieve total response in the face of
traditional arts which focus on narrower inlets
of sensation.

• •

Multimedias are invariably sad comedies. They
work as a kind of colorful group therapy, a
woeful mating of actors and viewers, a mutual
semimasturbation. The performers seem to need
their audience and the spectators—the spectators
would find these same mild titillations in a freak
show or Fun Fair and fancier, more complete
amusements in a Mexican cathouse.

Novices, we watch the moves of silkworms who excite
their bodies in moist leaves and weave wet nests
of hair and skin.

This is a model of our liquid resting world
dissolving bone and melting marrow
opening pores as wide as windows.

The "stranger" was sensed as greatest menace
in ancient communities.

Metamorphose. An object is cut off from its name, habits, associations. Detached, it becomes only the thing, in and of itself. When this disintegration into pure existence is at last achieved, the object is free to become endlessly anything.

The subject says "I see first lots of things
which dance . . . then everything becomes gradually
connected."

Objects as they exist in time the clean eye and
camera give us. Not falsified by "seeing."

When there are as yet no objects.

Early film makers, who—like the alchemists—
delighted in a willful obscurity about their craft,
in order to withhold their skills from profane
onlookers.

     • •

Separate, purify, reunite. The formula of
Ars Magna, and its heir, the cinema.

     • •

The camera is androgynous machine, a kind of
mechanical hermaphrodite.

In his retort the alchemist repeats the work of
Nature.

Few would defend a small view of Alchemy as "Mother
of Chemistry," and confuse its true goal with those
external metal arts. Alchemy is an erotic science,
involved in buried aspects of reality, aimed
at purifying and transforming all being and matter.
Not to suggest that material operations are ever
abandoned. The adept holds to both the mystical
and physical work.

The alchemists detect in the sexual activity of man a correspondence with the world's creation, with the growth of plants, and with mineral formations. When they see the union of rain and earth, they see it in an erotic sense, as copulation. And this extends to all natural realms of matter. For they can picture love affairs of chemicals and stars, a romance of stones, or the fertility of fire.

Strange, fertile correspondence the alchemists
sensed in unlikely orders of being. Between
men and planets, plants and gestures, words and
weather. These disturbing connections: an in-
fant's cry and the stroke of silk; the whorl
of an ear and an appearance of dogs in the yard;
a woman's head lowered in sleep and the morning
dance of cannibals; these are conjunctions which
transcend the sterile signal of any "willed"
montage. These juxtapositions of objects, sounds,
actions, colors, weapons, wounds, and odors shine
in an unheard-of way, impossible ways.

Film is nothing when not an illumination of
this chain of being which makes a needle poised
in flesh call up explosions in a foreign capital.

Cinema returns us to anima, religion of matter,
which gives each thing its special divinity and
sees gods in all things and beings.

Cinema, heir of alchemy, last of an erotic science.

Surround Emperor of Body.
Bali Bali dancers
Will not break my temple.

Explorers
suck eyes into the head.

The rosy body cross
secret in flow
controls its flow.

Wrestlers
in body weights dance
and music, mimesis, body.

Swimmers
entertain embryo
sweet dangerous thrust flow.

The Lords. Events take place beyond our knowledge
or control. Our lives are lived for us. We can
only try to enslave others. But gradually, special
perceptions are being developed. The idea of the
"Lords" is beginning to form in some minds. We
should enlist them into bands of perceivers to
tour the labyrinth during their mysterious noc-
turnal appearances. The Lords have secret entrances,
and they know disguises. But they give themselves
away in minor ways. Too much glint of light in
the eye. A wrong gesture. Too long and curious a
glance.

The Lords appease us with images. They give us
books, concerts, galleries, shows, cinemas. Es-
pecially the cinemas. Through art they confuse
us and blind us to our enslavement. Art adorns
our prison walls, keeps us silent and diverted
and indifferent.

Dull lions prone on a watery beach.
The universe kneels at the swamp
to curiously eye its own raw
postures of decay
in the mirror of human consciousness.

Absent and peopled mirror, absorbent,
passive to whatever visits
and retains its interest.

Door of passage to the other side,
the soul frees itself in stride.

Turn mirrors to the wall
in the house of the new dead.

THE NEW CREATURES

To Pamela Susan

I

Snakeskin jacket
Indian eyes
Brilliant hair

He moves in disturbed
Nile Insect
Air

II

You parade thru the soft summer
We watch your eager rifle decay
Your wilderness
Your teeming emptiness
Pale forests on verge of light
decline.

More of your miracles
More of your magic arms

III

Bitter grazing in sick pastures
Animal sadness & the daybed
Whipping.
Iron curtains pried open.
The elaborate sun implies
dust, knives, voices.

Call out of the Wilderness
Call out of fever, receiving
the wet dreams of an Aztec King.

IV

The banks are high & overgrown
rich w/ warm green danger.
Unlock the canals.
Punish our sister's sweet playmate distress.
Do you want us that way w/ the rest?
Do you adore us?
When you return will you
      still want to play w/ us?

V

Fall down.
Strange gods arrive in fast enemy poses.
Their shirts are soft marrying
    cloth and hair together.
All along their arms ornaments
    conceal veins bluer than blood
    pretending welcome.
Soft lizard eyes connect.
Their soft drained insect cries erect
    new fear, where fears reign.
The rustling of sex against their skin.
The wind withdraws all sound.
Stamp your witness on the punished ground.

VI

Wounds, stags, & arrows
Hooded flashing legs plunge
      near the tranquil women.
Startling obedience from the pool people.
Astonishing caves to plunder.
Loose, nerveless ballets of looting.
Boys are running.
Girls are screaming, falling.
The air is thick w/ smoke.
Dead crackling wires dance pools
      of sea blood.

VII

Lizard woman
w/ your insect eyes
w/ your wild surprise.
Warm daughter of silence.
Venom.
Turn your back w/ a slither of moaning wisdom.
The unblinking blind eyes
      behind walls new histories rise
and wake growling & whining
        the weird dawn of dreams.
Dogs lie sleeping.
The wolf howls.
A creature lives out the war.
A forest.
A rustle of cut words, choking
river.

VIII

The snake, the lizard, the insect eye
the huntsman's green obedience.
Quick, in raw time, serving
     stealth & slumber,
grinding warm forests into restless lumber.

Now for the valley.
Now for the syrup hair.
Stabbing the eyes, widening skies
behind the skull bone.
Swift end of hunting.
Hug round the swollen torn breast
     & red-stained throat.
The hounds gloat.
Take her home.
Carry our sister's body, back
to the boat.

A pair of Wings
Crash
High winds of Karma

Sirens

Laughter & young voices
in the mts.

Saints
the Negro, Africa
Tattoo
        eyes like time

Build temporary habitations, games
& chambers, play there, hide.

First man stood, shifting stance
while germs of sight
unfurl'd Flags in his skull

and quickening, hair, nails, skin
turned slowly, whirl'd, in
the warm aquarium, warm
wheel turning.

Cave fish, eels, & gray salamanders
turn in their night career of sleep.

The idea of vision escapes
the animal worm whose earth
is an ocean, whose eye is its body.

The theory is that birth is prompted
by the child's desire to leave the womb.
But in the photograph an unborn horse's
neck strains inward w/ legs scooped out.

From this everything follows:

Swallow milk at the breast
until there's no milk.

Squeeze wealth at the rim
until tile pools claim it.

He swallows seed, his pride
until w/ pale mouth legs

she sucks the root, dreading
world to devour child.

Doesn't the ground swallow me
when I die, or the sea
if I die at sea?

The City. Hive, Web, or severed
insect mound. All citizens heirs
of the same royal parent.

The caged beast, the holy center,
a garden in the midst of the city.

"See Naples & die."
Jump ship. Rats, sailors
& death.

So many wild pigeons.
Animals ripe w/ new diseases.
"There is only one disease
and I am its catalyst,"
cried doomed pride of the carrier.

Fighting, dancing, gambling,
bars, cinemas thrive
in the avid summer.

Savage destiny

Naked girl, seen from behind,

on a natural road

Friends
explore the labyrinth

—Movie
young woman left on the desert

A city gone mad w/ fever

Sisters of the unicorn, dance
Sisters & brothers of Pyramid
Dance

Mangled hands
Tales of the Old Days
Discovery of the Sacred Pool
changes
Mute-handed stillness baby cry

The wild dog
The sacred beast

Find her!

He goes to see the girl
of the ghetto.
Dark savage streets.
A hut, lighted by candle.
She is magician
Female prophet
Sorceress
Dressed in the past
All arrayed.

The stars
The moon
She reads the future
in your hand.

The walls are garish red
The stairs
High discordant screaming
She has the tokens.
"You too"
"Don't go"
He flees.
Music renews.

The mating-pit.
"Salvation"
Tempted to leap in circle.

Negroes riot.

Fear the Lords who are secret among us.
The Lords are w/ in us.
Born of sloth & cowardice.

He spoke to me. He frightened
me w/ laughter. He took
my hand, & led me past
silence into cool whispered
Bells.

A file of young people
going thru a small woods

They are filming something
in the street, in front of
our house.

Walking to the riot
Spreads to the houses
the lawns
      suddenly alive now
      w/ people
      running

I don't dig what they did
to that girl
Mercy pack
Wild song they sing
As they chop her hands
Nailed to a ghost
Tree

I saw a lynching
Met the strange men
        of the southern swamp
Cypress was their talk
Fish-call & bird-song
Roots & signs
        out of all knowing
They chanced to be there
Guides, to the white
gods.

An armed camp.
Army army
burning itself in
feasts.

Jackal, we sniff after the survivors of caravans.
We reap bloody crops on war fields.
No meat of any corpse deprives our lean bellies.
Hunger drives us on scented winds.
Stranger, traveler,
peer into our eyes & translate
the horrible barking of ancient dogs.

Camel caravans bear
witness guns to Caesar.
Hordes crawl & seep inside
the walls. The streets
flow stone. Life goes
on absorbing war. Violence
kills the temple of no sex.

Terrible shouts start
       the journey
—If they had migrated sooner

—a high wailing keening
piercing animal lament
from a woman
high atop a Mt. tower

—Thin wire fence
in the mind
dividing the heart

Surreptitiously
They smile
Inviting—Smiling

       Choktai
       leave!
       evil
       leave!
       No come here
       Leave her!

A creature is nursing
its child
soft arms around
the head & the neck
a mouth to connect
leave this child alone
This one is mine
I'm taking her home
Back to the rain

The assassin's bullet
Marries the King
Dissembling miles of air
To kiss the crown.
The Prince rambles in blood.
Ode to the neck
That was groomed
For rape's gown.

Cancer city
Urban fall
Summer sadness
The highways of the old town
Ghosts in cars
Electric shadows

Ensenada
the dead seal
the dog crucifix
ghosts of the dead car sun.
Stop the car.
Rain. Night.
Feel.

Sea-bird sea-moan
Earthquake murmuring
Fast-burning incense
Clamoring surging
Serpentine road
To the Chinese caves
Home of the winds
The gods of mourning

The city sleeps
& the unhappy children
roam w/ animal gangs.
They seem to speak
to their friends
the dogs
who teach them trails.
Who can catch them?
Who can make them come
inside?

The tent girl
at midnight
stole to the well
& met her lover there
They talked a while
& laughed
& then he left
She put an orange pillow
on her breast

In the morning
Chief w/drew his troops
& planned a map
The horsemen rose on up
The women fixed the ropes
on tight
The tents are folded now
We march toward the sea

Catalog of Horrors
Descriptions of Natural disaster
Lists of miracles in the divine corridor
Catalog of fish in the divine canal
Catalog of objects in the room
List of things in the sacred river

I

The soft parade has now begun
on Sunset.
Cars come thundering down
the canyon.
Now is the time & the place.
The cars come rumbling.
"You got a cool machine."
These engine beasts
muttering their soft
talk. A delight
at night
to hear their quiet voices
again
after 2 years.

Now the soft parade
has soon begun.
Cool pools
from a tired land
sink now
in the peace of evening.

Clouds weaken
& die.
The sun, an orange skull,
whispers quietly, becomes an
island, & is gone.

There they are
watching
us everything
will be dark.
The light changed.
We were aware
knee-deep in the fluttering air
as the ships move on
trains in their wake.
Trench mouth
again in the camps.
Gonorrhea
Tell the girl to go home
We need a witness
to the killing.

II

The artists of Hell
set up easels in parks
the terrible landscape,
where citizens find anxious pleasure
preyed upon by savage bands of youths

I can't believe this is happening
I can't believe all these people
are sniffing each other
& backing away
teeth grinning
hair raised, growling, here in
the slaughtered wind

I am ghost killer.
witnessing to all
my blessed sanction

This is it
no more fun
the death of all joy
has come.

Do you dare
deny my
potency
my kindness
or forgiveness?
Just try
you will fry
like the rest
in holiness

And not for a
penny
will I spare
any time
for you
Ghost children
down there
in the frightening world

You are alone
& have no need of other
you & the child mother
who bore you
who weaned you
who made you man

-booth killer
ₗle bandit
ₜraight from ambush

Kill me!
Kill the child who made
Thee.
Kill the thought-provoking
senator of lust
who brought you to this state.

Kill hate
disease
warfare
sadness

Kill badness
Kill madness

Kill photo mother murder tree
Kill me.
Kill yourself
Kill the little blind elf.

The beautiful monster
vomits a stream of watches
clocks jewels knives silver
coins & copper blood

The well of time & trouble
whiskey bottles perfume
razor blades beads
liquid insects hammers
& thin nails the feet of
birds eagle feathers & claws
machine parts chrome
teeth hair shards of
pottery & skulls the ruins
of our time the debris by
a lake the gleaming
beer cans & rust & sable
menstrual fur

Dance naked on broken
bones feet bleed & stain
glass cuts cover your mind
& the dry end of vacuum
boat while the people
drop lines in still pools
& pull ancient trout

from the deep home. Scales
crusted & gleaming green
A knife was stolen. A
valuable hunting knife
By some strange boys
from the other camp across
the Lake

I

Are these our friends
racing & shuddering
thru the calm vales of parliament

My son will not die in the war
He will return
numbed peasant voice of Orient
fisherman

Last time you said
this was the only way
voice of tender young girl

Running & speaking
infected green
jungles

consult the oracle
bitter creek
crawl
they exist on rainwater

monkey-love
mantra mate
maker of brandy

isles
ɔn

this thin granule
evil snakeroot
from the southern
shore

way out miracle
will find thee

The chopper blazed over
inward click & sure
blasted matter, made
the time bombs free
of leprous lands
spotted w/ hunger
& clinging to law

Please
show us your ragged head
& silted smiling eyes
calm in fire
a silky flowered shirt
edging the eyes, alive
spidery, distant
dial lies

come, calm one
into the life-try

already wifelike
latent, leathery, loose
lawless, large & languid
She was a kingdom-cry
legion of lewd marching
mind-men

Where are your manners
out there on the sunlit
desert
boundless galaxies of dust
cactus spines, beads
bleach stones, bottles
& rust cars, stored for shaping

The new man, time-soldier
picked his way narrowly
thru the crowded ruins
of once grave ctiy, gone
comic now w/ rats
& the insects of refuge

He lives in cars
goes fruitless thru
the frozen schools
& finds no space
in shades of obedience

rs are silenced
graveled guard-towers
on the westward beach
red of watching

if only one horse were left
to ride thru the waste
a dog at his side
to sniff meat-maids
chained on the public poles

there is no more argument
in beds, at night
blackness is burned
Stare into the parlors of town
where a woman dances
in her European gown
to the great waltzes
this could be fun
to rule a wasteland

II

Cherry palms
Terrible shores
& more
& many more

This we know
that all are free
in the school-made
text of the unforgiven

deceit smiles
incredible hardships are suffered
by those barely able
to endure

but all will pass
lie down in green grass
& smile, & muse, & gaze
upon her smooth
resemblance
to the mating-Queen
who it seems
is in love
w/ the horseman

now, isn't that fragrant
Sir, isn't that knowing
w/ a wayward careless
backward glance

July 24, 1968
Los Angeles, The United States, Hawaii